BIG ENGLISH 2

T0346033

Contents

In My Classroom

1 Listen and number.

2 Look at 1. Circle.

1 They're **colouring** / **counting**.

2 She's **writing** / **playing a game**.

3 They're **using the computer** / **listening**.

4 She's **gluing** / **counting**.

5 He's **writing** / **using the computer**.

6 He's **cutting** / **watching a DVD**.

3 Listen and sing. Then match and write.

a

_____

b

_____

Here's My Classroom!

Look! Here's my classroom.
And here are my friends!
Peter, Sarah and Timothy,
Penny, Jack and Jen!

Peter is cutting paper.
Penny is writing her name.
Sarah is listening to a story.
And Jack is playing a game.

Timothy is counting.
Jen is gluing.
We have fun and learn a lot.
What are your friends doing?

c

_____

d

_____

4 Draw your classroom. Then say.

5 **Read and write.**

What's Maria Doing?

What's Maria doing?

She's cutting paper.

No, she isn't. She's using the computer.

No, she isn't. Look.

Now Maria is writing on the board.

Maria

1 How many Marias are there in the class?

There are _____ Marias.

2 What is one Maria doing?

She's _____ and

_____.

3 What is the other Maria doing?

She's _____.

THINK BIG **What do you like doing? Read and circle.**

using the computer   writing   reading

listening   cutting   gluing

watching a DVD   playing a game

6 Look and match. Then say.

1 What's she doing?

She's listening to a story.

2 What are they doing?

They're watching a DVD.

3 What's he doing?

He's gluing shapes.

7 Listen. Follow the path.

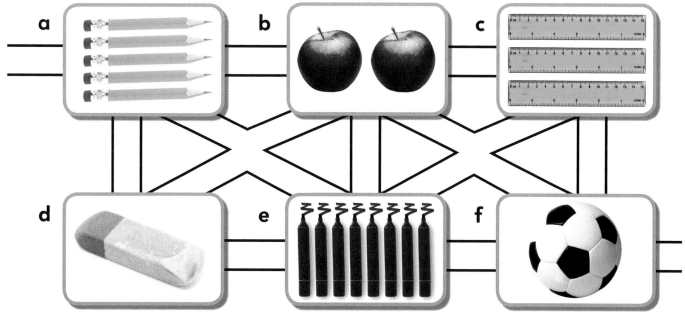

8 **Look and write.**

are they (x2)   He's (x2)   She's   They're (x2)   What's he (x2)   What's she

1 What _____ doing? _____ listening.

2 _____ doing? _____ cutting.

3 _____ doing? _____ colouring.

4 What _____ doing? _____ playing a game.

5 _____ doing? _____ counting.

9 **Look at 8. Read and ✓.**

1 There are ☐ one ball.   ☐ four backpacks.

2 There's ☐ one ball.   ☐ four backpacks.

10 **Write the word and the number.**   equals (x2)   minus   plus

1

 + =

6 pencils _____ 6 pencils _____ ☐ pencils.

2

 – =

10 footballs _____ 5 footballs _____ ☐ footballs.

11 **Write +, – or = and the number.**

1

 minus equals ☐ apples.

14 apples   8 apples

2

 plus  equals ☐ marker pens.

10 marker pens   2 marker pens

12 **Write +, –, = and the numbers. Then do the sums.**

1 sixty plus seven equals _____

2 eighty six minus three equals _____

 Write. What two things do you count every day in your classroom?

13 **Read and match. Then say.**

a

1 May I use the marker pens now?

b

2 Yes, let's take turns!

c

3 It's fun taking turns!

14 **Find and write the sentences.**

1 computer   May   now?   the   use   I

_____

2 turns!   let's   Yes,   take

_____

3 fun   taking   It's   turns.

_____

15 **Find and circle the letters th.**

16 **Read and circle the letters th.**

1 bath **2** path **3** this **4** that

17 **Match the words with the same sounds.**

1 they **a** thin
2 Maths **b** then

18 **Listen and chant.**

There are three
Crocodiles in the bath.
They've got thin mouths
But big teeth!
Look out! Look out!

19 **Look and write.**

counting   cutting   playing a game   using the computer

1 What's she doing?

She's _____.

2 What's he doing?

He's _____.

3 What are they doing?

They're _____.

4 What are they doing?

They're _____.

20 **Count and write the numbers. Circle There's or There are.**

Our Classroom	
computer	l
chairs	lllll lllll lllll lll
rubbers	lllll lll
desks	lllll llll
teacher	l

1 There's / There are ____ computer.

2 There's / There are ____ chairs.

3 There's / There are ____ rubbers.

4 There's / There are ____ desks.

5 There's / There are ____ teacher.

21 **Find the words. Circle.**

colouring   counting   cutting   gluing   listening   writing

e	s	g	l	u	i	n	g	m	c
m	i	n	g	i	l	u	r	e	o
n	g	a	t	f	a	s	g	k	u
g	o	t	a	l	k	i	n	g	n
c	o	l	o	u	r	i	n	g	t
u	n	g	t	u	n	g	l	d	i
t	g	o	i	f	g	a	u	g	n
t	l	i	s	t	e	n	i	n	g
i	s	w	r	i	t	i	n	g	a
n	p	a	e	n	t	t	g	i	t
g	i	f	o	i	a	s	f	n	o

22 **Circle and write.**

1 11 marker pens **+** / **–** ☐ marker pens = 7 marker pens

2 18 pencils **+** / **–** ☐ pencils = 20 pencils

3 13 books **+** / **–** ☐ books = 1 book

23 **What are you doing in the classroom? Draw and write.**

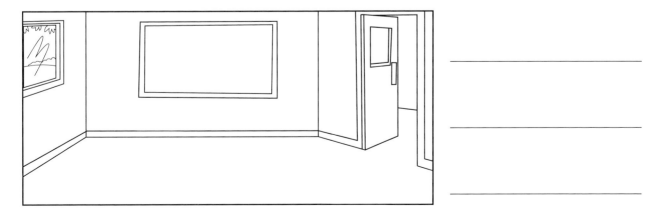

_____

_____

_____

My Games

1 **Read and match. Then say.**

a

1 doing gymnastics

2 flying kites

b

c

3 ice skating

d

4 skateboarding

5 playing tennis

e

f

6 climbing trees

2 Listen and sing. Then match.

a **b**

c **d**

Come On and Play

We're playing in the playground.
There are a lot of games to play.
Football, tennis and volleyball.
What do you want to play today?

Paul likes playing on the swings.
Emma likes running and climbing.
We all love riding our bikes.
Tell us! What do you like doing?

We're playing in the playground.
It's always so much fun.
Come on and play with us.
We play with everyone!

3 Draw. Then say.

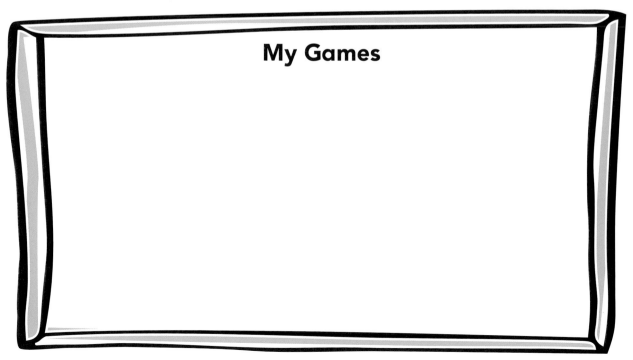

My Games

4 Read and write.

We Like Playing Together!

I like playing football. My sister loves skateboarding.

What does your brother like doing?

He loves playing volleyball.

We like playing together, too.

How can you do that?

1 What does Jamie like doing?

He likes _____.

2 What does Jenny love doing?

She loves _____.

3 What does Tony love doing?

He loves _____.

4 What do they all like doing?

They like _____.

THINK BIG **Circle the odd one out.**

1:32

5 **Write do or does. Then listen and match.**

1 What _____ he love doing?

2 What _____ they like doing?

3 What _____ she like doing?

4 What _____ they love doing?

a

b

c

d

6 **Look at 5. Write the answers.**

1 He loves _____.

2 They like _____.

3 She likes _____.

4 They love _____.

7 **Read and ✓.**

a   b

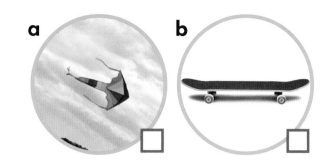

1 I like skateboarding.

a   b

2 He loves playing tennis.

a   b

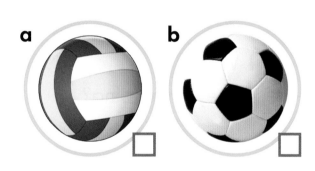

3 They like playing volleyball.

a   b

4 She likes climbing trees.

8 **Look at 7. Write the questions.**

1 _____

2 _____

3 _____

4 _____

9 **Look and match. Colour the bones.**

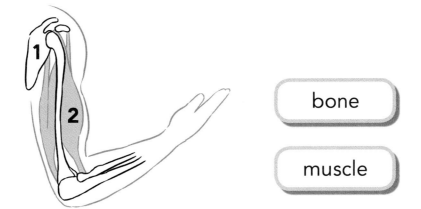

bone

muscle

10 **Listen and circle.**

1
| 3 | 13 |
| 34 | 43 |

2
| 7 | 27 |
| 37 | 72 |

3
| 3 | 13 |
| 30 | 33 |

4
| 6 | 16 |
| 26 | 62 |

THINK BIG **What parts of our body do we use when ice skating? Tick (✓).**

bones ☐   legs ☐   nose ☐

arms ☐   mouth ☐   muscles ☐

11 **Read and match.**

1

a

Always wear a helmet and knee pads.

2

b

Always put one leg on each side.

3

c

Always sit down on the swing.

4

d

Always slide with your feet in front of you.

12 **Find and circle the letters ng and nk.**

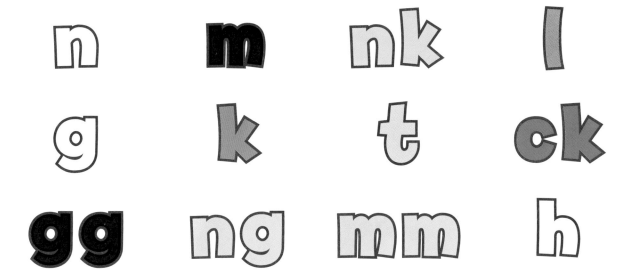

n m nk l

g k t ck

gg ng mm h

13 **Read and circle the letters ng and nk.**

1 ring **2** pink **3** bang **4** ink

14 **Match the words with the same sounds.**

1 wing   **a** sink

2 bank   **b** sing

1:43

15 **Listen and chant.**

Sing a song about a king.
Thank you! Thank you!
He's got a big pink ring
And big blue wings.
Thank you! Thank you!

16 Look and write.

1 What does she love doing? She loves _____.

2 What _____ he like doing? He likes
_____.

3 What does he _____? He
_____.

4 What does she love _____? She
_____.

17 **Read and write.**

bones   feet   hands   kick

1 We kick with our _____.

2 One hand has got 27 _____.

3 When we _____ a ball, we use 13 muscles.

4 We throw with our _____.

18 **Find and write the words.**

1 _____   gindo   stcsimygan

2 _____   ngilfy   sktie

3 _____   gniblcim   rsete

4 _____   eic   ingastk

5 _____   npialgy   sitnen

6 _____   dirgni   kisbe

19 **Draw and write.**

What do you love doing?

I love _____.

In My House

1 **Look and write the names of the rooms. Then match.**

bathroom
bedroom
kitchen
living room

bed
chair
cupboard
dressing table
fridge
table
TV
shelf
sofa

2 **Look at 1. What's in the rooms? Write.**

1 There's a _____, a _____ and a _____
in the bedroom.

2 There's a _____, a _____ and a _____
in the living room.

3 There's a _____, a _____ and a _____
in the kitchen.

3 **Listen and sing. Circle the pictures from the song.**

Where Are My Keys?

Where are my keys, Mum?
Your keys are on the chair.
The chair? Which chair?
There are chairs everywhere!

There's a chair in the living room,
And one in the bedroom, too.
There are chairs in the dining room.
I don't know which chair. Do you?

Your keys are where you left them.
Put on your glasses and see.
They're on the chair behind you.
My keys are there! Silly me!

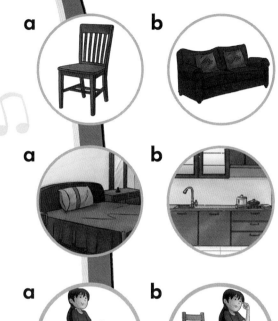

4 **Look in your house. Count and write the number.**

1 There are _____ chairs in the living room.

2 There are _____ chairs in the bedroom.

3 There are _____ chairs in the kitchen.

4 There are _____ chairs in the dining room.

5 **Read and circle.**

1 The boys are Jamie's **brothers** / **cousins**.

2 The boys' mother is Jamie's **aunt** / **uncle**.

3 The boys are in the **bedroom** / **kitchen**.

4 The TV is in the **kitchen** / **living room**.

THINK BIG

Count and write the number.

How many cousins have you got? ☐

How many aunts have you got? ☐

How many uncles have you got? ☐

6 **Read and match.**

1 in front of   **2** between   **3** next to   **4** behind

a 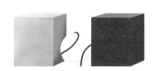   **b**    **c**   **d**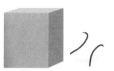

7 **Follow, write and circle.**

chair(x2)   kitchen   sofa

1 _____ the table?

_____ **next to / behind**

the _____ .

2 _____ my keys?

_____ **in front of /**

behind the _____ .

3 _____ his shoes?

_____ **on / between**

the _____ .

4 _____ the cooker?

_____ **in / in front of**

the _____ .

a

b

c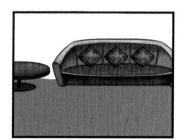

d

8 **Look and write. Use 's.**

1 Dan /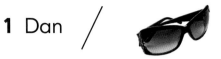

They're _____.

2 Suzie /

It's _____.

3 my mum /

It's _____.

4 her brother /

It's _____.

9 **Read the puzzles. Look at 8. Then write.**

1 It's behind the table, next to the chair. What is it?

_____

2 It's on the table, between the lamp and the bike. What is it?

_____

3 They're on the chair behind the kite. What are they?

_____

4 It's on the dressing table, next to the backpack. What is it?

_____

10 **Write the names of the objects. Then write old or new.**

These things are _____.

These things are _____.

_____

_____

_____

_____

_____

_____

11 **Look, read and ✓.**

1   This bath is new. ☐   This bath is old. ☐

2   This jacket is new. ☐   This jacket is old. ☐

3   This is a new phone. ☐   This is an old phone. ☐

4   These are new skates. ☐   These are old skates. ☐

THINK **BIG**   **Draw one old thing and one new thing in your house.**

12 **Listen and number. Then say.**

1:56

a

b

c

I put my dirty dishes in the sink.

I put my dirty clothes in the washing machine.

I put my toys in the toy box.

13 **Find and write the words.**

1 _____   xbo   yot

2 _____   niks

3 _____   ngihsaw   hcamein

14 **How do you keep your bedroom tidy? Draw and write.**

I _____.

15 **Find and circle the letters oo.**

16 **Read and circle the letters oo.**

1 moon   **2** book   **3** zoo   **4** foot

17 **Match the words with the same sounds.**

1 food   **a** look
2 good   **b** cool

18 **Listen and chant.**

Look in my
Cook book.
The food is good!
The food is cool!

19 **Look and write.**

| bath | bed | chair | cooker | fridge | lamp | sink | TV |

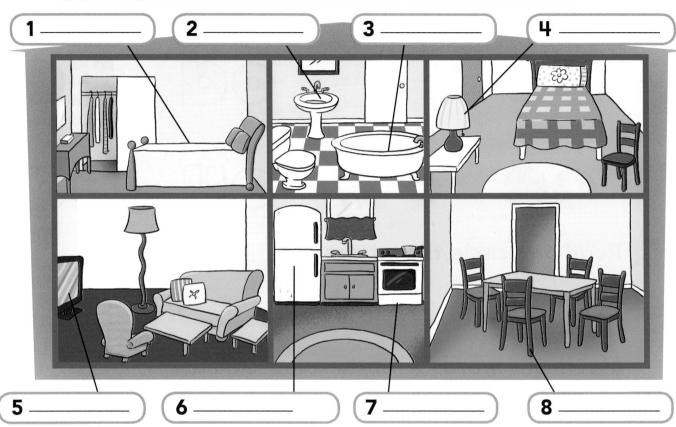

1 _____
2 _____
3 _____
4 _____

5 _____
6 _____
7 _____
8 _____

20 **Look at 19. Match.**

1 Where's the cooker? a They're in the dining room.

2 Where's the bath? b It's in the kitchen next to the sink.

3 Where are the chairs? c It's in the bathroom.

21 **Look at 19. Write.**

1 What's in the bedroom?

There's a _____, a _____, a _____ and a _____.

2 What's in the living room?

There's a _____, a _____, a _____ and a _____.

22 **Look and write. Where is Milo?**

| behind | between | in front of | next to |

1 _____

2 _____

3 _____

Let's play hide-and-seek!

4 _____

23 **Look, read and circle.**

1 This computer is **old** / **new**.

2 These chairs are **new** / **old**.

3 This is an **old** / **new** phone.

4 These cars are **old** / **new**.

24 **Draw a living room. Where's the DVD player?**

THINK BIG

1 **Look, find and number.** 🔍

2 **Look and find. Circle.**

At your school:
What do you like doing in the classroom? Circle one activity in red.

In your house:
What have you got in your bedroom? Circle one thing in blue.

3 **Think, look and draw.**

One thing is in the bedroom, in the classroom and in the playground. What is it?

🔍 **MY CLASSROOM**

1 cutting

2 gluing

3 using the computer

MY GAMES

4 playing on the seesaw

5 playing on the slide

6 playing on the swing

MY HOUSE

7 a bed

8 a dressing table

9 a lamp

In My Town

1 **Look and match.**

1 shopping centre

2 train station

3 cinema

4 bank

5 restaurant

6 supermarket

2 Listen and sing. Circle the places on the map.

Maps Are Great!

Where's the bookshop?
I want to buy a book.
Here, I've got a map.
Come on. Let's take a look!

The bookshop is in River Street.
It isn't far from us.
Do you want to walk there?
No, thanks! Let's take the bus!

I want to send a letter, too.
Is there a post office? Do you know?

I'm looking at the map. Yes, there is.
It's near the bookshop. Come on. Let's go.

Maps are really great.
I use them every day.
In town or out of town
They help me find my way!

River Street

Maple Street

Bookshop

Train Station

Music Shop

Computer Shop

Main Street

Post Office

Park Street

Restaurant

Bus

Elm Street

3 What's in your town? Tick (✓).

☐ bookshop   ☐ post office   ☐ bus stop

☐ petrol station   ☐ computer shop

4 Read and ✓.

What's in the shopping centre?

☐ There's a bookshop.

☐ There's a cinema.

☐ There's a computer shop.

☐ There are restaurants.

☐ There are supermarkets.

THINK BIG **What is there in your town? Read and circle.**

bank   bus stop   computer shop

petrol station   shopping centre

train station

5 **Look and write want to or wants to.**

me   Amy   Lisa   my brother

1 I _____ eat pizza.

2 Amy _____ go to the supermarket.

3 Lisa _____ buy a computer.

4 My brother _____ send a letter.

6 **Write.**

the bookshop, the cinema

the petrol station, the bank

I want to go _____ _____.

I _____ _____ _____.

Mum wants to _____ _____.

She _____ _____ _____.

7 **Draw a post office and a bookshop.**

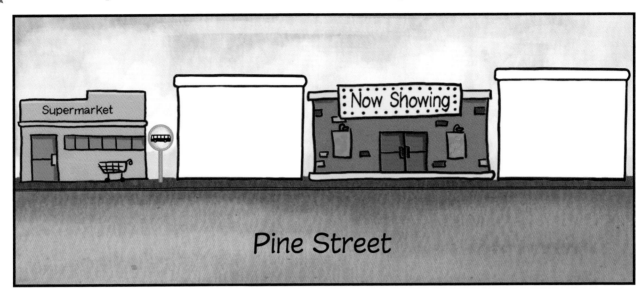

8 **Look at 7. Write Yes, there is or No, there isn't.**

1 Is there a bus stop in Pine Street?

_____

2 Is there a train station in Pine Street?

_____

3 Is there a supermarket next to the post office?

_____

4 Is there a cinema between the post office and the bookshop?

_____

5 Is there a petrol station near the bus stop?

_____

6 Is there a restaurant next to the cinema?

_____

9 Look, read and write.

bike   boat   bus   train

1 In London, some children go to school by _____.

2 In Mexico City, many children go to school by _____.

3 In Bangkok, many children go to school by _____.

4 In Beijing, many children go to school by _____.

10 Draw and write.

I go to school by _____.

THINK BIG How do teachers go to school in your country? Tick (✓).

boat ☐   train ☐   bus ☐   bike ☐   car ☐

11 **Read, look and circle.**

a

1 I **look / don't look** left,
then right, then left again
before I cross the road.

b

2 I wait for the **blue / green**
man.

c

3 I **always / never** cross at
the pedestrian crossing.

12 **Find and write the words.**

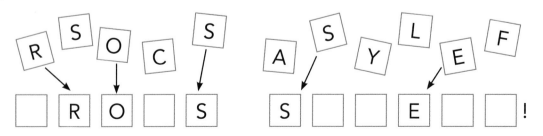

13 **Find and circle the letters ai and oa.**

14 **Read and circle the letters ai and oa.**

1 rain 2 coat 3 train 4 boat

15 **Match the words with the same sounds.**

1 road **a** wait

2 tail **b** soap

16 2:18 **Listen and write the letters. Then chant.**

Wear a c_____ t

To s_____ l the b_____ t!

Drive the tr_____ n,

In the r_____ n!

17 Listen and follow the path.

18 Look at **17**. Write.

Where do they go?

1 _____ 2 _____

3 _____ 4 _____

5 _____

19 **Write want to or wants to. Then match.**

1 We _____ buy fruit.

2 She _____ go by train.

3 You _____ go to the bank.

4 He _____ buy petrol.

a There's a bank in Elm Street.

b Is there a petrol station near here?

c There's a supermarket behind the shopping centre.

d Is there a train station in London Road?

20 **Look, read and circle.**

1 In Mexico City, many children go to school by **bus** / **boat**.

2 In China, many children go to school by **train** / **bike**.

3 In London, many children go to school by **boat** / **train**.

4 In Bangkok, many children go to school by **boat** / **bike**.

21 **Draw your favourite shop. Where is it?**

It's _____

_____.

unit 5

My Dream Job

1 **Circle and match.**

a	p	e	o	c	k	a
d	s	i	n	g	e	r
o	p	b	l	d	w	t
c	i	v	r	o	t	i
t	s	i	e	d	t	s
o	v	p	r	t	s	t
r	h	a	c	t	o	r

pilot

artist

singer

actor

vet

doctor

2 **Look and circle.**

1 chef / writer

2 athlete / dancer

44 Unit 5

3 Listen and chant. Then write.

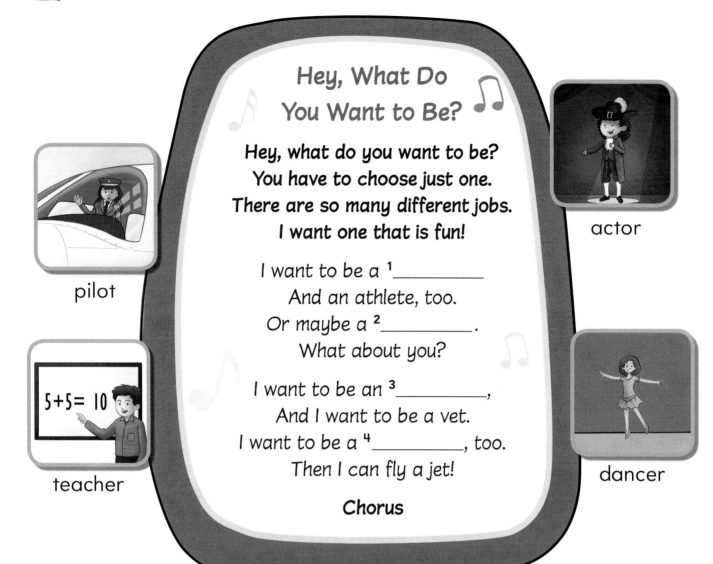

Hey, What Do You Want to Be?

Hey, what do you want to be?
You have to choose just one.
There are so many different jobs.
I want one that is fun!

I want to be a ¹_____
And an athlete, too.
Or maybe a ²_____.
What about you?

I want to be an ³_____,
And I want to be a vet.
I want to be a ⁴_____, too.
Then I can fly a jet!

Chorus

pilot

teacher

actor

dancer

4 Write and draw.

I want to be **a / an**
_____.

5 **Read and circle.**

1 Jenny wants to be a **singer** / **writer**.

2 Dan wants to be a **writer** / **singer**.

3 Jenny and Dan are talking to their **friend** / **teacher**.

6 **Read the story again. What do they like doing? Match.**

1 eating

2 dancing

3 singing

4 writing

THINK BIG **Read and circle. I like music. I want to be a _____ and a _____.**

chef   dancer   singer   writer

7 **Look and write.**

drawing   flying   singing   writing

1 What do you want to be?

I _____ to be a singer. I like _____.

2 What do you want to be?

_____ an artist. I like _____.

3 What do you want to be?

_____ a pilot. I _____.

4 What do you want to be?

_____

_____

8 **What do you like doing? Write and draw.**

I like _____

_____.

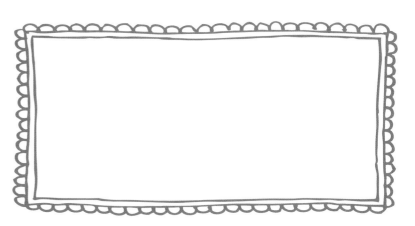

9 **Look and write.**

1

_____?
She wants to be a dancer.

2

_____?
He wants to be a teacher.

3

_____?
She wants to be a doctor.

4

_____?
He wants to be an athlete.

10 **Look and match. Then write.**

| cooking   running |

1 What does he want
to be?

2 What does she want
to be?

a She wants to be a chef.
She likes _____.

b He wants to be an athlete.
He likes _____.

11 **Write. What do you want to be? Why?**

_____

_____

_____

12 Look and circle.

1 park ranger / lifeguard

2 lifeguard / farmer

3 park ranger / nurse

4 farmer / nurse

2:31

13 Listen and write. Then match.

1 A _____ helps people in the water.

2 A _____ protects animals.

3 A _____ helps ill people.

4 A _____ grows food for people to eat.

a

b

c

d

THINK BIG **Read, guess and write.**

doctor   teacher   vet

1 I help people in hospitals. Who am I? _____

2 I help sick animals. Who am I? _____

3 I help children to learn. Who am I? _____

14 **Look, write and match.**

1 I like Art.

a

I want to be a

_____.

2 I like Science.

b

I want to be an

_____.

3 I like Maths.

c

I want to be a

_____.

4 I like Music.

d

I want to be a

_____.

15 **Find and write the sentences.**

1 Maths. I like _____

2 I be to a want teacher. _____

3 I Art. like _____

4 writer. want a to be I _____

16 **Find and circle the letters ar, er and or.**

17 **Read and circle the letters ar, er and or.**

1 arm   **2** corn   **3** teacher   **4** car

18 **Match the words with the same sounds.**

1 singer   **a** for
2 born   **b** art
3 cart   **c** letter

19 **Listen and write the letters. Then chant.**

2:37

I want to be a sing _____

_____ an artist painting _____ t.

I want to be a teach _____

Or a farmer with a c _____ t!

20 **Look and write. What do they want to be?**

actor	artist	dancer	pilot
singer	doctor	teacher	vet

ACROSS ➡

1   4   7   8

DOWN ⬇

2   3   5   6

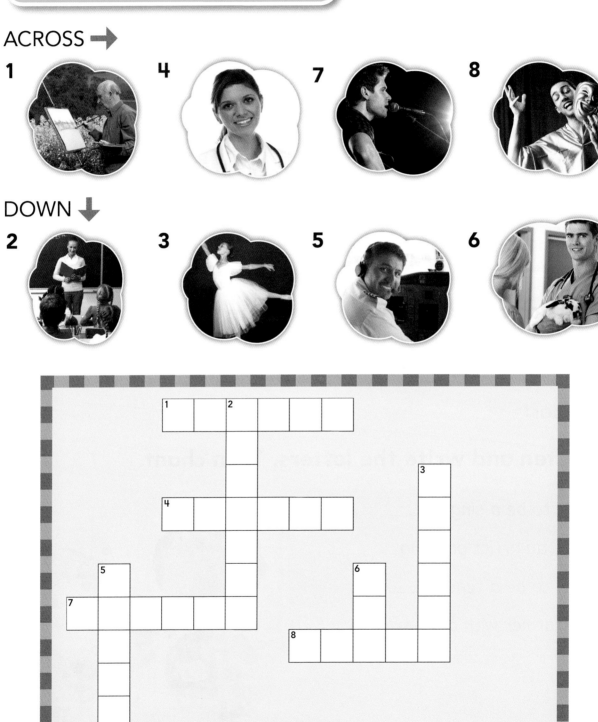

21 **Look and write.**

1 What does she want to be?

_____

2 What does he want to be?

_____

3 What does she want to be?

_____

4 What does he want to be?

_____

22 **Read and write.**

farmer   lifeguard   nurse   park ranger

1 A _____ protects animals.

2 A _____ helps ill people.

3 A _____ grows food.

4 A _____ helps people in the water.

unit 6 **My Day**

1 Listen and ✓. Then write.

1 a  **b**
☐ ☐

_____

2 a  **b**
☐ ☐

_____

3 a  **b**
☐ ☐

_____

4 a  **b**
☐ ☐

_____

2 Read, draw and say.

1

one o'clock

2

ten o'clock

3 Listen and sing. Look at the pictures. Then number in order.

a

b

What Time Is It?

Tick, tock. It's seven o'clock.
Time to get up and get dressed.
I want to stay in bed.
But it's time to brush my teeth!

Tick, tock. It's eight o'clock.
At nine o'clock I start school.
I eat my breakfast and get my books.
I love school, it's cool!

c

Tick, tock. It's three o'clock.
There's no more school today.
I do my homework and I go out.
And there's my friend to play.

d

Now it's evening and it's eight o'clock
And it's time to go to bed.
I watch TV and read my book.
Time to sleep now, good night!

4 Look at 3. Write.

1 I get up at _____.

2 I start school at _____.

3 I go out at _____.

4 I go to bed at _____.

5 **Read. Then write in order.**

Max's Day

Max gets up at two o'clock in the afternoon. Then he eats and goes out.

When does Max come back?

He comes back at seven o'clock. Then he sleeps again.

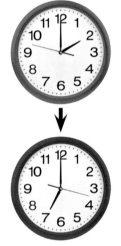

1 _____

2 _____

3 _____

4 _____

5 _____

Max comes home.

Max eats.

Max gets up.

Max goes out.

Max sleeps again.

THINK BIG

How many hours do I sleep?

I go to bed at _____ in the evening.
I get up at _____ in the morning.
I sleep for _____ hours.

2:47

6 Listen and write.

1 get up: _____

2 start school: _____

3 finish school: _____

4 go out: _____

5 watch TV: _____

6 go to bed: _____

7 Look at 6. Write.

1 When do you get up?

2 When ____ you start school?

3 When _____ finish school?

4 _____ go out?

5 _____ TV?

6 _____

1 I get up at _____.

2 I _____ at _____.

3 I _____ at _____.

4 _____ at _____.

5 _____

6 _____

8 **Read and circle. Then draw and write the time.**

1 When **do** / **does** she go out?
She **go out** / **goes out** at 4:00.

_____

2 When **do** / **does** he watch TV?
He **watch** / **watches** TV at 5:00.

_____

3 When **do** / **does** you go to bed?
I **go to bed** / **goes to bed** at 8:00.

_____

4 When **do** / **does** they get up?
They **get up** / **gets up** at 7:00.

_____

5 When **do** / **does** this film start?
It **start** / **starts** at 10:00.

_____

6 When **do** / **does** this film finish?
It **finish** / **finishes** at 12:00.

_____

9 Read and write. Then match.

| glass | sand | sun | time | two | water |

1 A sundial uses the _____ to tell the time. The sun makes a shadow on the sundial. The shadow tells the _____ of day.

a

2 An hourglass uses _____ to tell the time. Sand falls from the top of a _____ to the bottom.

b
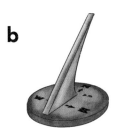

3 A water clock uses _____ to tell the time. It works like an hourglass. It's got _____ cups. The water falls from one cup to the other.

c

Write the times.

THINK BIG

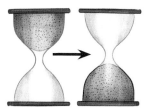
2:00   3:00

1
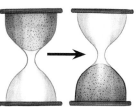
10:00   _____

2
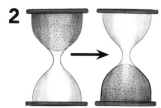
_____   7:00

10 **School starts at 8:00. Help Anna get to school on time. Follow the paths and choose 😊 or 🙁.**

a

She gets up at six o'clock.

She eats breakfast at seven o'clock.

She gets to school at eight o'clock.

b

She gets her backpack ready the night before school.

She brushes her teeth at nine o'clock.

She gets to school at ten o'clock.

11 **How do you get to school on time? Tick (✓) and draw one step.**

☐ I get up early on school days.

☐ I get dressed quickly and eat breakfast.

☐ I get my backpack ready the night before school.

☐ I always get to school on time.

12 **Find and circle the letters ch, tch and sh.**

13 **Read and circle the letters ch, tch and sh.**

1 ship   **2** chin   **3** witch   **4** fish   **5** rich

14 **Match the words with the same sounds.**

1 match   **a** shop
2 chip   **b** watch
3 dish   **c** lunch

15 **Listen and write the letters. Then chant.**

Watch the wi_____,

She's having lun_____!

Fi_____ and _____ ips,

At the _____ op!

16 **Write the words. Then colour the times.**

| brushes – **green** | finishes – **brown** | o'clock – **orange** |
| school – **blue** | six – **purple** | snack – **red** |

1 I start _____ at nine o'clock.

2 He _____ his teeth at eight o'clock.

3 The film _____ at five o'clock.

4 They eat a _____ at four o'clock.

5 She reads a book at seven _____ .

6 I eat chicken and salad at _____ o'clock.

17 **Look and write.**

1 When _____ they go out?

They _____ at _____ .

2 When _____ she get up?

She _____ at _____ .

3 When _____ he start school?

He _____ at _____ .

18 **Write about you. Add the times.**

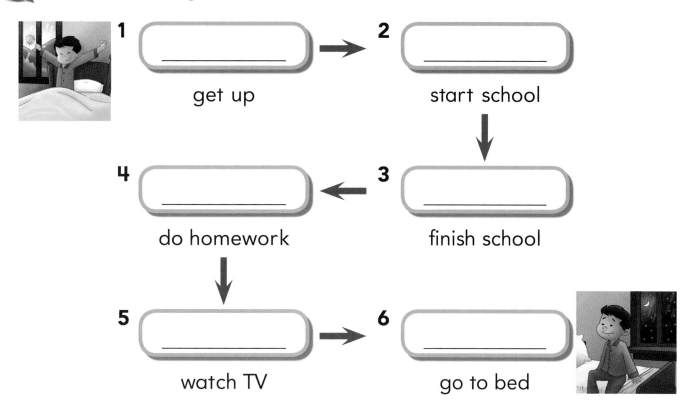

1 get up → 2 start school

4 do homework ← 3 finish school

5 watch TV → 6 go to bed

19 **Look at 18. Write.**

1 When do you get up?

_____

2 When do you start school?

_____

3 When do you finish school?

_____

4 When do you do your homework?

_____

5 When do you watch TV?

_____

6 When do you go to bed?

_____

TH■NK BIG

1 **Look, find and number.** 🔍

2 **Mark is visiting a small town. What can he do? Look at the town and ✓.**

Mark's To-Do List

- ☐ buy a book
- ☐ go to a restaurant
- ☐ send a letter
- ☐ buy fruit
- ☐ watch a film

3 **Think and draw. In the town, there isn't a _____ .**

🔍 **MY TOWN**

1 bus stop

2 computer shop

3 supermarket

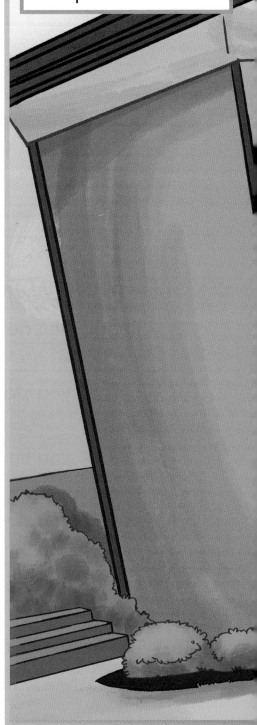

🔍 **DREAM JOBS**

4 artist

5 doctor

6 athlete

🔍 **MY DAY**

7 brush teeth

8 get up

9 go to bed

unit 7 My Favourite Food

1 **Look and match.**

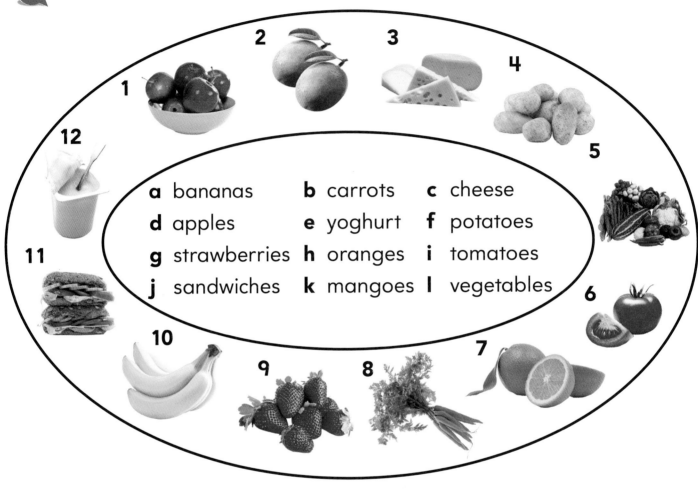

a bananas   b carrots   c cheese
d apples   e yoghurt   f potatoes
g strawberries h oranges   i tomatoes
j sandwiches   k mangoes   l vegetables

2 **Look and write.**

I like _____ and
_____. I don't
like _____.

3 Listen and sing. Match and write.

a

b

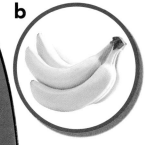

Let's Eat Lunch!

It's twelve o'clock.
Let's eat lunch.
Do you like bananas?
I like them for lunch!

Do you like tomatoes?
Yes, I do. I like tomatoes. I really do.
Do you like potatoes?
Yes, I do. I like potatoes, too.
Do you?

Meat and fruit,
Vegetables and snacks,
I like them all.
Can I have more please?

Have some chips
And a burger, too.
Let's share some ice cream.
I like eating lunch with you!

c

d

e

f

4 Write and draw.

What do you want?

I want _____.

5 **Read. Then circle T for true or F for false.**

Do You Like Fruit?

It's four o'clock, boys. Do you want a snack?

Yes, please, Dad.

But I don't like bananas.

Jamie doesn't like bananas, either.

Do you like mangoes?

Yes, I do. I like mangoes.

1 It's six o'clock.   T F

2 Dan and Jamie want a snack.   T F

3 Dan likes bananas.   T F

4 Jamie doesn't like bananas.   T F

5 Dan likes mangoes.   T F

THINK BIG

Circle the fruit.

mangoes

bananas

carrots   oranges

apples

potatoes

meat

6 **What do you like? Listen and circle.**

1 a  b

2 a  b

3 a  b

4 a   b

7 **Look and write.**

1

I like _____
_____.
I don't like _____.

2

I like _____.
I don't like _____
_____.

3

I like _____
_____.
I don't like _____.

4

I like _____.
I don't like _____
_____.

8 Look and circle.

1

Do / Does she like strawberries?
Yes, she **do / does**.

2

Do / Does he like tomatoes?
No, he **don't / doesn't**.

3

Do / Does they like sandwiches?
Yes, they **do / does**.

4

Do / Does they like cheese?
No, they **don't / doesn't**.

9 Match. Then write.

1 Do you like meat? **a** 😊 Yes, he _____.

2 Do they like vegetables? **b** ☹ No, I _____.

3 Does he like burgers? **c** 😊 😊 Yes, they _____.

10 **Match.**

1 Pineapples   **a** come from China.

2 Watermelons   **b** come from South America.

3 Kiwis   **c** come from Mexico.

4 Avocados   **d** come from Africa.

Read and guess the fruit.

1 It's big and green on the outside and pink on the inside. What is it? _____

2 It's small and brown on the outside and green on the inside. What is it? _____

3 It's yellow and it's got green leaves. What is it? _____

4 It's green and it's got a big seed inside. What is it? _____

11 **Look and circle.**

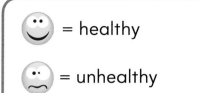 = healthy

= unhealthy

1

salad

2

crisps

3

biscuits

4

carrots

5

chocolate

6

apples

12 **Find and write the sentences.**

1 one Just please. biscuit,

_____

2 thanks. No me, crisps for

_____

13 **Find and circle the letters ee and ie.**

14 **Read and circle the letters ee and ie.**

1 bee   **2** tie   **3** sheep   **4** pie

15 **Match the words with the same sounds.**

1 lie   **a** feet
2 see   **b** cried

3:19
16 **Listen and write the words. Then chant.**

" **1** _____ the **2** _____!"

3 _____ the **4** _____.

" **5** _____ the **6** _____!"

7 _____ the **8** _____.

Review

17 **What do you like? Look and write five foods.**

1 _____

2 _____

3 _____

4 _____

5 _____

18 **Look and write.**

1

Does she like bananas?

2

He _____ carrots.

He _____ cheese.

3

Does she like snacks?

_____.

She _____ meat.

4

They _____ cheese.

They _____

sandwiches.

19 **Look and write.**

Anna	☺	☺	☹	☺
Ruben	☹	☺	☹	☺
Mary	☺	☹	☺	☹
You	◯	◯	◯	◯

☺ = like

☹ = doesn't like

1 _____ Anna _____ tomatoes?

_____

2 _____ Ruben _____ strawberries?

_____

3 _____ Mary _____ potatoes?

_____

4 _____ Mary and Ruben _____ burgers?

_____

5 _____ you _____ burgers?

_____

20 **Circle and answer about you.**

1 Does your **mum / friend / brother** like vegetables?

_____

2 Do your **parents / friends / brothers** like mangoes?

_____

3 Does your **dad / friend / sister** like oranges?

_____

Wild Animals

1 Look and write.

cheetahs   giraffes   hippos   kangaroos
monkeys   polar bears   zebras

ZOO

1 _____

2 _____

3 _____

4 _____

5 _____

6 _____

7 _____

2 Look and match.

1 crocodile   **2** parrot   **3** snake   **4** peacock

a    b    c    d

3 Listen and sing. Write the words.

kangaroo

elephant

monkey

polar bear

To the Zoo!

I really like animals!
Do you like them, too?
That's why I'm so happy.
We're going to the zoo!

A ¹_____ can jump.
A ²_____ can jump, too.
Crocodiles can chase and swim.
And you, what can you do?

A ³_____ can't fly or jump up high.
An ⁴_____ can't climb trees.
Fish can't run and hippos can't fly.
Come and see them.
Oh, yes, please!

Now it's time to say goodbye
To every animal here.
But we can come back
And see them every year!

4 What animals do you like seeing at the zoo?

_____   _____   _____

_____   _____   _____

5 **Read and circle.**

1 **Monkeys** / **Hippos** can climb trees.

2 **Monkeys** / **Hippos** can eat a lot of food.

3 **Monkeys** / **Hippos** can jump.

4 **Monkeys** / **Hippos** have got big mouths.

5 **Jamie** / **Jenny** can eat a lot.

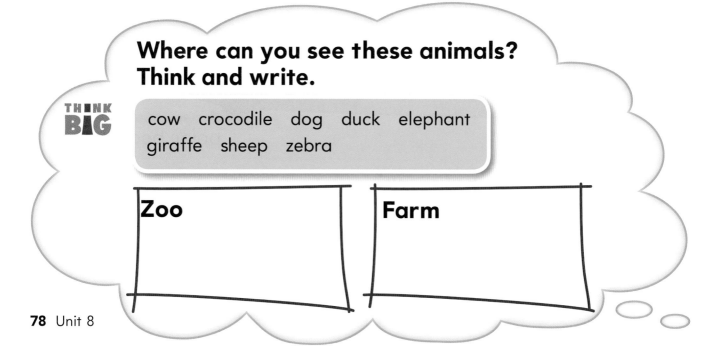

Where can you see these animals? Think and write.

THINK BIG

cow   crocodile   dog   duck   elephant
giraffe   sheep   zebra

Zoo

Farm

6 **Read and answer. Follow the correct path to the zoo.**

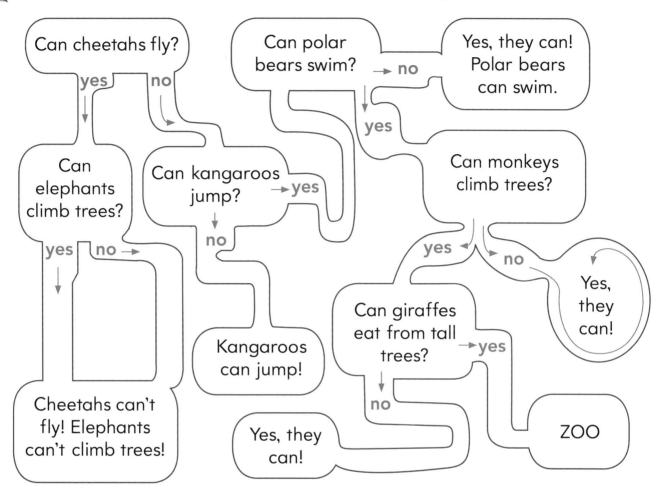

7 **Match and write. Use can or can't.**

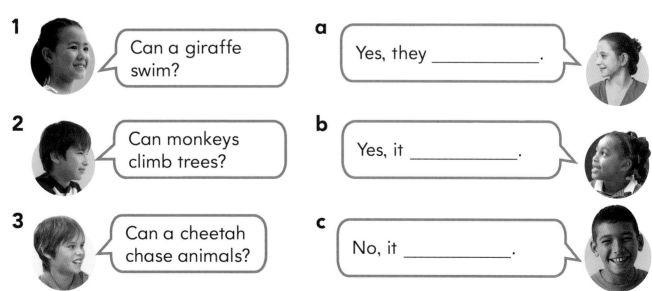

1 Can a giraffe swim?

a Yes, they _____.

2 Can monkeys climb trees?

b Yes, it _____.

3 Can a cheetah chase animals?

c No, it _____.

8 **Look at the chart. Write questions and answers.**

	run	jump	climb trees	catch animals
1 giraffes	yes	no	no	no
2 polar bears	yes	yes	yes	yes
3 hippos	yes	no	no	no
4 cheetahs	yes	yes	yes	yes
5 zebras	yes	yes	no	no
6 kangaroos	no	yes	no	no

1 _____ run?

_____ , they _____ .

2 _____ jump?

_____ , they _____ .

3 _____ climb trees?

_____ , they _____ .

4 _____ catch animals?

_____ , they _____ .

5 _____ run?

_____ , they _____ .

6 _____ climb trees?

_____ , they _____ .

9 Write. Then read and match.

| desert | forest | jungle | ocean |

1 _____

2 _____

3 _____

4 _____

a Deer live in forests.

b Lizards live in deserts.

c Fish live in oceans.

d Parrots live in jungles.

THINK BIG **Circle the odd one out. Which animals live in oceans?**

fish   lizard   seal   shark   whale

10 **Look, listen and write.**

1 I like peacocks.
They're so _____.

2 Monkeys are so
_____.

3 Giraffes are _____.
Their necks are so long.

4 Elephants are very
_____.

11 **Find and write the describing words.**

1 _____ z a a m n g i

2 _____ v r e e c l

3 _____ f l u t i u e b a

4 _____ o g n t s r

12 **Find and circle the letters ou and ow.**

13 **Read and circle the letters ou and ow.**

1 you **2** owl **3** soup **4** cow

14 **Match the words with the same sounds.**

1 down   **a** route

2 group   **b** town

15 **Listen and write the words. Then chant.**

An ¹_____ went
²_____ to ³_____
To see a ⁴_____ of
⁵_____ drinking
⁶_____.

16 Look and write.

ACROSS ➡

3   5   6

DOWN ⬇

1   2   4

17 Write. Then match questions and answers.

1 _____ a monkey climb trees?

a No, they _____.

2 _____ parrots fly?

b Yes, it _____.

3 _____ a peacock swim?

c Yes, they _____.

4 _____ snakes run?

d No, it _____.

18 **Look and circle.**

1 elephant / hippo **2 giraffe / crocodile** **3 lizard / snake**

19 **Read and write.**

| deserts | forests | jungles | oceans |

1 Foxes live in _____.

2 Whales live in _____.

3 Lizards live in _____.

4 Monkeys live in _____.

20 **Draw your favourite animal. Then write.**

What is it? _____

Can it climb trees? _____

Can it chase animals? _____

Can it _____? _____

unit 9 Fun All Year

1 Number the months in order.

April

SUN	MON	TUE	WED	THU	FRI	SAT
1	2	3	4	5	6	7
8	9	10	11	12	13	14
15	16	17	18	19	20	21
22	23	24	25	26	27	28
29	30					

January

SUN	MON	TUE	WED	THU	FRI	SAT
1	2	3	4	5	6	7
8	9	10	11	12	13	14
15	16	17	18	19	20	21
22	23	24	25	26	27	28
29	30	31				

May

SUN	MON	TUE	WED	THU	FRI	SAT
	1	2	3	4	5	
6	7	8	9	10	11	12
13	14	15	16	17	18	19
20	21	22	23	24	25	26
27	28	29	30	31		

August

SUN	MON	TUE	WED	THU	FRI	SAT
		1	2	3	4	
5	6	7	8	9	10	11
12	13	14	15	16	17	18
19	20	21	22	23	24	25
26	27	28	29	30	31	

July

SUN	MON	TUE	WED	THU	FRI	SAT
1	2	3	4	5	6	7
8	9	10	11	12	13	14
15	16	17	18	19	20	21
22	23	24	25	26	27	28
29	30	31				

November

SUN	MON	TUE	WED	THU	FRI	SAT
		1	2	3		
4	5	6	7	8	9	10
11	12	13	14	15	16	17
18	19	20	21	22	23	24
25	26	27	28	29	30	

December

SUN	MON	TUE	WED	THU	FRI	SAT
						1
2	3	4	5	6	7	8
9	10	11	12	13	14	15
16	17	18	19	20	21	22
23	24	25	26	27	28	29
30	31					

June

SUN	MON	TUE	WED	THU	FRI	SAT
					1	2
3	4	5	6	7	8	9
10	11	12	13	14	15	16
17	18	19	20	21	22	23
24	25	26	27	28	29	30

October

SUN	MON	TUE	WED	THU	FRI	SAT
	1	2	3	4	5	6
7	8	9	10	11	12	13
14	15	16	17	18	19	20
21	22	23	24	25	26	27
28	29	30	31			

February

SUN	MON	TUE	WED	THU	FRI	SAT
		1	2	3	4	
5	6	7	8	9	10	11
12	13	14	15	16	17	18
19	20	21	22	23	24	25
26	27	28				

March

SUN	MON	TUE	WED	THU	FRI	SAT
				1	2	3
4	5	6	7	8	9	10
11	12	13	14	15	16	17
18	19	20	21	22	23	24
25	26	27	28	29	30	31

September

SUN	MON	TUE	WED	THU	FRI	SAT
						1
2	3	4	5	6	7	8
9	10	11	12	13	14	15
16	17	18	19	20	21	22
23	24	25	26	27	28	29
30						

2 Write the month.

1 This month has got five letters.

This month is before April.

_____

2 This month has got six letters. This month is after July.

_____

3 This month has got eight letters.

This month is between October and December.

_____

3 **Listen and chant. Then write.**

> ### I Like July!
>
> **1**_____ is my favourite month.
> I like **2**_____, too.
> I'm happy and on holiday,
> There is so much to do!
>
> I also like **3**_____.
> That's when I start school.
> I'm so excited, aren't you?
> My friends will be there, too!
>
> I don't like **4**_____.
> It is so very cold.
> But then it is my birthday, too.
> This year I'm eight years old!

August

July

December

September

4 **What month do you like? Write. Then circle how many days it's got.**

_____

M	T	W	T	F	S	S
		1	2	3	4	5
6	7	8	9	10	11	12
13	14	15	16	17	18	19
20	21	22	23	24	25	26
27	28	29	30	31		

5 **Read and write.**

1 Jenny's favourite month is _____.

2 Jenny _____ goes on holiday in December.

3 Dan _____ goes on holiday in winter.

4 It's too _____.

 THINK BIG

What do you do in December?

I always _____ in December.

I never _____ in December.

6 **Look at the calendar. Then write and circle.**

June

Sun	Mon	Tues	Wed	Thur	Fri	Sat
				1	2	3
4	5	6	7	8	9	Visit Cousins 10
11	12	13	14	Sally's party 15	16	17
Father's Day 18	19	20	21	22	23	Beach 24
25	26	27	28	29	30	

1 Do you have a New Year's party in June?

No, I _____ . I **always** / **never** have a New Year's party in June.

2 What do you do in June?

I **always** / **never** visit my cousins in June.

3 What do you celebrate in June?

We **always** / **never** celebrate Father's Day in June.

4 Do you have Billy's party in June?

No, we _____ . We **always** / **never** have his party in June.

5 Do you go to the beach in June?

Yes, we _____ . We **always** / **never** go to the beach in June.

7 **Answer about you. Write and circle.**

Do you go on holiday in June?

_____ , I _____ . I **always** / **never** go on holiday in June.

8 **Look and write always or never.**

Hi, I'm Julia. I always go ice skating in winter.

	winter	spring	summer	autumn
always	go ice skating	have a party	go to the beach	visit my cousins
never	ride my bike	go on holiday	go to school	celebrate New Year's

1 What does she do in winter?

She _____ rides her bike. She _____ goes ice skating.

2 What does she do in spring?

She _____ has a party. She _____ goes on holiday.

3 What does she do in summer?

She _____ goes to the beach. She _____ goes to school.

4 What does she do in autumn?

She _____ celebrates New Year's. She _____ visits her cousins.

9 **Choose a season. Then write.**

What do you do in _____?

I always _____. I never _____.

3:49

10 **Listen and write. Then match. Write the number.**

England   China   Japan

December   May   July   October

1 In _____, children like celebrating the mid-Autumn festival. This festival is in September or _____.

2 In _____, children celebrate the star festival on the seventh of _____.

3 Children in _____ celebrate spring on the first of _____.

4 People all over the world celebrate New Year's Eve on the last day of _____.

THINK BIG **What do you do on New Year's Eve?**

On New Year's Eve, I _____.

11 Read, look and match.

1 In spring, he rides his bike.

a

2 In summer, she likes to swim in the sea.

b

3 In autumn, they rake leaves.

c

4 In winter, they skate on ice.

d

12 Find and write the words. Then match each season to the months in your country.

1 t n r e w i _____

a December, January, February

2 r p s g n i _____

b March, April, May

3 u t a n u m _____

c June, July, August

4 m r e u s m _____

d September, October, November

13 **Write the alphabet in the correct order.**

Aa | ___ | ___ | __d | ___ | F_ | ___ | __h | I __

Q_ | ___ | O_ | ___ | M_ | ___ | __k | ___

___ | __t | ___ | V_ | ___ | __x | Y_ | ___

14 **Listen and write the letters and words. Then chant.**

A, B, C, ¹____, E, ²____, G.
I can see an ant and a ³_____.
What can you see?
H, I, ⁴____, K, L, ⁵____, N, O, ⁶____.
I can see a ⁷_____ and some ink. What can you see?
Q, ⁸____, S, T, ⁹____, V.
I can see a ¹⁰_____ and a snake.
What can you ¹¹_____?
W, ¹²____, Y and ¹³____.
I can see ¹⁴_____ yellow wolves
and a ¹⁵_____, I said!

15 **Follow the maze. Write the months in order.**

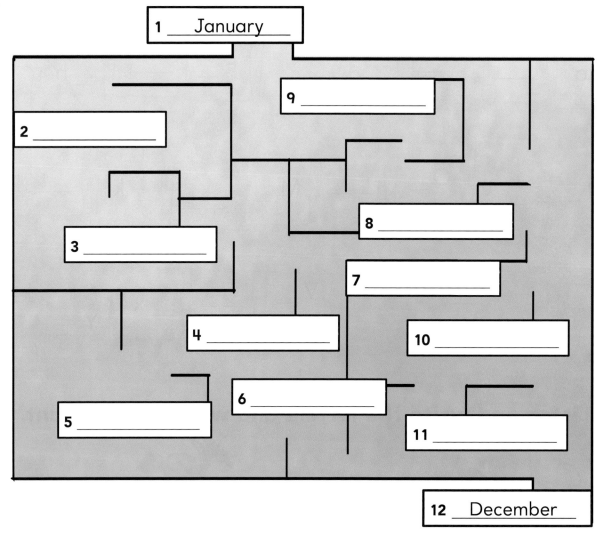

1 ___January___

9 _____

2 _____

8 _____

3 _____

7 _____

4 _____

10 _____

6 _____

5 _____

11 _____

12 ___December___

16 **Complete the dialogue.**

| always | Do | don't |
| never | What | |

Maria: ¹_____ do you do in winter?

Peter: We ²_____ go ice skating.

Maria: We always visit our cousins in winter. We ³_____ go ice skating.

Peter: ⁴_____ you go to the beach in summer?

Maria: No, we don't. We ⁵_____ go to the beach in summer. We always go to the swimming pool and eat ice cream!

17 **Listen and circle. Then match.**

1 They **always** / **never** have a New Year's party in winter.

2 He **always** / **never** goes on holiday in autumn.

3 I **always** / **never** swim in spring.

4 She **always** / **never** goes to school in summer.

a

b

c

d

18 **Draw and write about you.**

1 What do you always do in autumn?

_____

_____

2 What do you never do in spring?

_____

_____

THINK BIG

1 **Look, find and number.** 🔍

2 **Look at 1 and write. Add one food word, one animal word and one month word.**

3 **Look at the table and circle one food in red:**

What do you like eating for lunch?

4 **Look at the table and circle one food in blue:**

What do you never eat for lunch?

5 **Think, look and circle in green.**

There's a hat on an elephant. That's silly. What other silly things can you see?

🔍 **FOOD**

1 carrots

2 cheese

3 bananas

_____

ANIMALS

4 zebra

5 elephant

6 giraffe

_____

MONTHS

7 summer month

8 winter month

9 autumn month

_____

What's he/she **doing**?   He's/She's **writing**.

What **are** they **doing**?   They're **gluing**.

1 **Circle the correct form of the verb. Then match.**

1 What **is / are** he doing?   **a** She's colouring.

2 What **is / are** they doing?   **b** They're watching a DVD.

3 What **is / are** she doing?   **c** He's counting.

How many pictures are there?   **There's** one picture.

How many books are there?   **There are** three books.

2 **Look and write. Use There's or There are.**

1 _____ one teacher.

2 _____ one book.

3 _____ three pupils.

> What **does** he/she **like doing**?　　He/She **likes skateboarding**.
>
> What **do** they **like doing**?　　They **like flying kites**.

1 **Circle the correct form of the verb.**

1 What **do** / **does** he like doing?

He **like** / **likes** playing tennis.

2 What **do** / **does** they like doing?

They **like** / **likes** climbing trees.

3 What **do** / **does** she like doing?

She **like** / **likes** doing gymnastics.

2 **Look and write the question. Then write the answer.**

listen　　use

1

What _____ doing?

He _____ the computer.

2

What _____ doing?

They _____.

Where**'s** the TV?	**It's** on the table.
Where **are** the chairs?	**They're** in the living room.

1 **Look. Write Where's or Where are.**

1 _____ the keys? **2** _____ the phone?

3 _____ the football? **4** _____ the skates?

2 **Look at 1. Answer the questions.**

1 _____ in the bedroom. **2** _____ on the bed.

3 _____ in the bath. **4** _____ next to the chair.

My mum**'s** phone is on the dressing table. Ben**'s** keys are on the table.

3 **Circle the correct word.**

1 Where are **Mum** / **Mum's** keys?

2 My **cousins** / **cousin's** are riding their bikes.

3 **Emily** / **Emily's** bedroom is next to the bathroom.

4 **Joes** / **Joe's** clothes are in the cupboard.

> I/We/They/You **want to** send a letter.   He/She **wants to** go to the bank.

1 **Circle the correct form of the verb.**

1 I **want** / **wants** to buy a book.

2 My aunt and uncle **want** / **wants** to go to a computer shop.

3 Julia **want** / **wants** to send a letter.

4 He **want** / **wants** to eat.

Is there a post office near here?	Yes, **there is**.
Is there a bank in Elm Street?	No, **there isn't**.

2 **Look and write.**

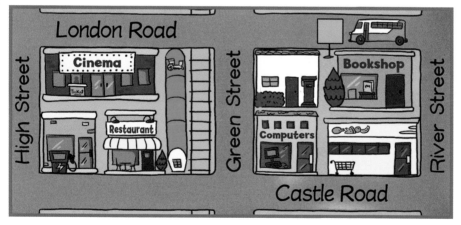

1 Is there a bookshop in High Street?

_____

2 Is there a computer shop in River Street?

_____

3 Where's the cinema? _____ a cinema near the train station?

_____

4 Let's eat. _____ a restaurant near here?

Yes, _____

What **do** you **want to be**?	I **want to be** an actor.
What **does** he/she **want to be**?	He/She **wants to be** a doctor.

1 Look and write.

1

What does he want to be?

He _____.

2

What does she want to be?

She _____.

3

_____?

She wants to be a pilot.

4

_____?

He wants to be a chef.

5

_____?

He _____.

6

What do you want to be?

_____

When **does** he/she **get up**?	He/She **gets up** at 6:00.
When **do** you/they **go to** bed?	I/They **go to** bed at 8:00.
When **does** the film **start**?	It **starts** at 7:00.

1 **Look and match. Then write the questions and answers.**

1 When

2 When

do
does

they go out?
she get up?
she go to bed?
school finish?

3 When

4 When

1 _____?

_____

2 _____?

_____

3 _____?

_____

4 _____?

_____

Do you **like** fruit?	Yes, I **do**. I like apples and bananas. No, I **don't**. I like cheese.
Do they **like** vegetables?	Yes, they **do**. They like carrots and potatoes. No, they **don't**. They like fruit.
Does he/she **like** fruit?	Yes, he/she **does**. He/She likes mangoes and oranges. No, he/she **doesn't**. He/She likes yoghurt.

1 **Circle the correct form of the verb.**

1 **Do** / **Does** she like meat?

No, she **don't** / **doesn't**. She likes sandwiches.

2 **Do** / **Does** they like snacks?

Yes, they **do** / **does**.

3 **Do** / **Does** she like cheese?

Yes, she **do** / **does**.

4 **Do** / **Does** they like tomatoes?

No, they **don't** / **doesn't**. They like potatoes.

5 **Do** / **Does** you like strawberries?

Yes, I **do** / **does**. I love strawberries!

2 **Look and write the questions and answers.**

1 you	bananas	🙁
2 Emma	oranges	😐
3 Sue and Hugo	vegetables	🙂

1 _____ you _____ bananas? _____

2 _____ she _____ oranges? _____

3 _____ they _____ vegetables? _____

| **Can** a kangaroo jump? | Yes, it **can**. | **Can** a snake jump? | No, it **can't**. |
| **Can** kangaroos jump? | Yes, they **can**. | **Can** snakes jump? | No, they **can't**. |

1 **Read. Circle T for true and F for false.**

1 Cheetahs can run.		T	F
2 A giraffe can fly.		T	F
3 A polar bear can jump.		T	F
4 An elephant can eat meat.		T	F
5 Hippos can climb trees.		T	F
6 Kangaroos can swim.		T	F

2 **Look at 1. Correct the false sentences. Use can't.**

1 _____

2 _____

3 _____

4 _____

3 **Write the questions. Use the words.
Then write the answer.**

chase	fly	talk	write

1 Can a cheetah _____ a zebra?   Yes, _____.

2 _____ a cheetah _____?   No, _____.

3 _____ cheetahs _____?   No, _____.

4 _____ cheetahs _____ their name? No, _____.

What does he/she do in January?	He/She **always** has a New Year's party in January.
Do you go on holiday in winter?	No, I/we don't. I/We **never** go on holiday in winter.

1 **Answer the questions about you. Circle the words.**

1 Do you do homework at six o'clock?

Yes / **No**. I **always** / **never** do homework at six o'clock.

2 Does your father like reading books?

Yes / **No**. He **always** / **never** reads books.

3 Do you like playing games at school?

Yes / **No**. I **always** / **never** play games at school.

4 Does your family watch DVDs on TV?

Yes / **No**. We **always** / **never** watch DVDs.

5 Does your mum eat meat?

Yes / **No**. She **always** / **never** eats meat.

2 **Look at the calendar. Write always or never.**

Anna: What does he do in January?

Bill: He _____ celebrates New Year's Day.

Anna: Does he celebrate New Year's in February, too?

Bill: No. He _____ celebrates New Year's in February! That's silly.

January

Sun	Mon	Tues	Wed	Thu	Fri	Sat
1 New Year's Day	2	3	4	5	6	7
8	9	10	11	12	13	14
15	16	17	18	19	20	21
22	23	24	25	26	27	28
29	30	31				

Write these words in your own language.

Unit 1	Page
classroom	4
colouring	4
counting	4
cutting	4
gluing	4
listening	4
playing a game	4
using the computer	4
watching a DVD	4
writing	4
one hundred	10
equals	10
minus	10
plus	10
take turns	12
bath	13
both	13
crocodile	13
Maths	13
mouth	13
path	13
teeth	13
then	13
thin	13
with	13

My favourite word:

Unit 2	Page
climbing trees	16
doing gymnastics	16
flying kites	16
ice skating	16
playing tennis	16
playing volleyball	16
riding my bike	16
skateboarding	16
like	17
love	17
playground	17
running	17
swing	18
together	18
team	19
muscles	22
bones	22
kick	22
take care of	22
throw	22
each side	24
helmet	24
in front of	24
knee pads	24
safely	24
slide	24

seesaw	24
bang	25
bank	25
ink	25
king	25
ring	25
sink	25
wing	25

My favourite word:

Unit 3	Page
bathroom	28
bed	28
bedroom	28
chair	28
cooker	28
cupboard	28
dressing table	28
DVD player	28
fridge	28
kitchen	28
lamp	28
living room	28
sofa	28
table	28
TV	28
behind	29

Wordlist

glasses	29	bookshop	44	pedestrian crossing	52
in	29	bus stop	44	right	52
keys	29	cinema	44	second	52
on	29	computer shop	44	ait	52
put on	29	petrol station	44	drive	53
aunt	30	post office	44	nail	53
cousin	30	restaurant	44	oak	53
uncle	30	shopping centre	44	rain	53
quiet	31	supermarket	44	sail	53
between	32	town	44	soap	53
next to	32	train station	44	tail	53
under	32	buy	45	wear	53
phone	33	eat	45	My favourite word:
new	34	far	45	
old	34	letter	45	**Unit 5** **Page**
skates	34	map	45	actor	56
dirty	36	near	45	artist	56
dishes	36	send	45	athlete	56
tidy	36	first	46	chef	56
toy box	36	hungry	46	dancer	56
washing machine	36	wallet	47	doctor	56
cook	37	film	48	dream job	56
cool	37	boat	50	pilot	56
moon	37	go to school by	50	singer	56
zoo	37	train	50	teacher	56
My favourite word:		cross the road	52	vet	56
		last	52	writer	56
Unit 4 **Page**		left	52	farmer	62
bank	44			grow	62

Wordlist

My BIG ENGLISH World

ACTIVITY BOOK 2

My name: _____

My age: _____

ME

FOLD

ENGLISH

AROUND ME

Paste or draw things with English words.

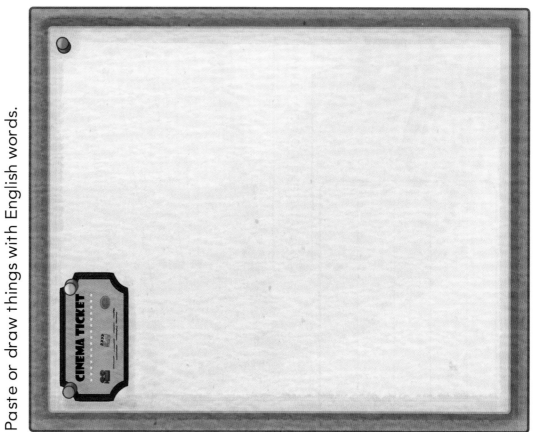

CINEMA TICKET

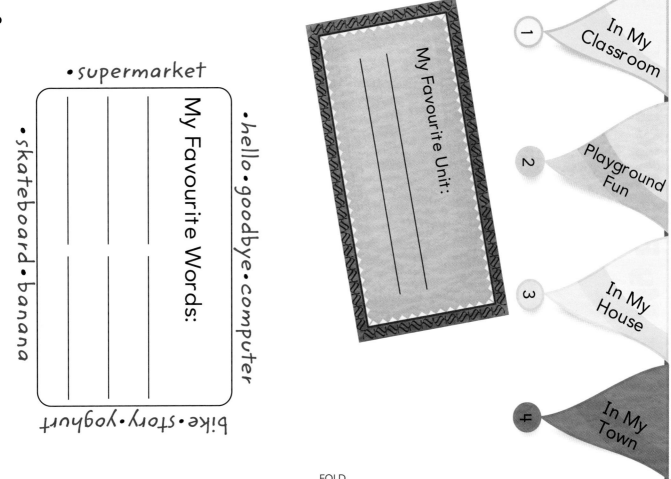

My Favourite Unit:

My Favourite Words:

• supermarket
• skateboard • banana
• hello • goodbye • computer
bike • story • yoghurt

1 In My Classroom

2 Playground Fun

3 In My House

4 In My Town

FOLD

My Favourite Project:

What do you like saying?

5 My Dream Job

6 My Day

7 Food

8 Wild Animals

9 Fun All Year